P9-AFC-453

The Ultimate DUCT TAPE BOOK

by Jim and Tim
the Duct Tape Guys

Pfeifer-Hamilton
Duluth, Minnesota

Pfeifer-Hamilton Publishers
210 West Michigan
Duluth, MN 55802-1908   218-727-0500

The Ultimate Duct Tape Book (Book 3)

© 1998 by Tim Nyberg Creative, Incorporated. All rights reserved. Except for short excerpts for review purposes, no part of this book may be reproduced or transmitted in any form by any means, electronic or mechanical, including photocopying, without permission in writing from the publisher.

Printed in the United States of America

10 9 8 7 6 5 4 3 2

Text: Jim Berg, Tim Nyberg, and Tony Dierckins
Design, illustrations, and photo manipulations: Tim Nyberg
Photographs: Erik Saulitis, Northwest Telecommunications

Library of Congress Cataloging in Publication Data
98-85758

ISBN 1-57025-171-1

3

Acknowledgments:

Hey, it's our third book! We couldn't have done it without the help of duct tape users around the world (you know who you are) who have shared their favorite duct tape uses with us. We wish we could give each of you credit for your suggestions, but many duct tape users supplied us with similar hints. So, we decided to leave each idea anonymous—that way you can impress your family and friends by claiming credit for any of them.

We also couldn't have done it without the help of our editor, Tony Dierckins, who we have now officially christened "The Third Duct Tape Guy." Hey, maybe we should start calling ourselves the Three Ducttapekateers—maybe not.

Thanks to our family and friends for their constant support (love can get you through times with no duct tape better than duct tape can get you through times with no love).

And last but not least, thanks to Pfeifer-Hamilton Publishers for enabling us to share the "Gospel of Duct Tape" with the world. May the tape be with you!

–Jim and Tim, the Duct Tape Guys

Blank Page

According to the *Chicago Manual of Style*, this page is traditionally left blank, but people have always told us that we have no style. So here is page IV (pronounced *ivy*) with some stuff on it, and some additional room for you to jot your own duct tape notes.

Notes:

Introduction:

The stuff in this, *The Ultimate Duct Tape Book*, has never appeared in book form before. EVER. Guaranteed. You may have seen it in one of our *365 Days of Duct Tape* Page-A-Day calendars (Workman Publishing). Or, you may have seen some of the hints if you have seen us perform at a home show, or have been watching us on television. But we know that calendar pages get ripped off and discarded, live appearances vanish forever, and television shows get vaporized and live out eternity floating around in the universe, so we felt obliged to package all of the hints never published in our first two books in this, the third and final book in the Duct Tape Trilogy.

We think John Madden said it best when he told us, "Where the hell would we be without duct tape?"

Hey, maybe that's how he makes those six-legged turkeys!

Enjoy!

—Jim and Tim, the Duct Tape Guys

Disclaimer:

Like our first two books, *The Duct Tape Book* and *Duct Tape Book Two—Real Stories*, this book contains humor. Please don't try any of the hints that seem blatantly stupid, potentially injurious, disrespectful to human or animal life, or outright dangerous. Some of the hints are real (we aren't distinguishing which ones). You may want to try some of these, or you may not. Whatever the case, you do so at your own risk. Other hints are merely for your entertainment (that is, of course, assuming you find extreme stupidity entertaining).

Naturally, all real brand names are the registered trademarks of their respective owners.

For best results, carry a roll of *REAL* duct tape with you at all times. For worst results, use processed cheese slices as an emergency substitute for duct tape.

–Jim and Tim, the Duct Tape Guys

3

Stop Smoking with The Duct Tape Patch

Trying to quit smoking? Just duct tape your cigarettes to your arm to create your own nonprescription nicotine Duct Tape Patch. Heavy smokers, soak 5–10 cigarettes in water, grind them into a paste, apply the goop to your upper arm, then secure the mixture with duct tape.

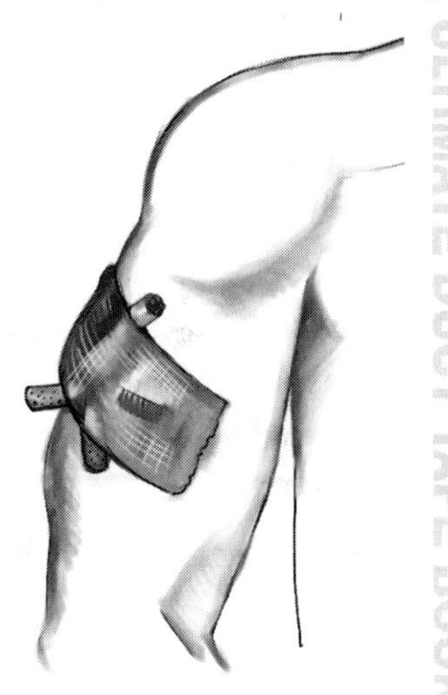

Duct Tape Patch II

Still smoking even though you've tried the Duct Tape Patch? Quit for good without gaining weight with the Duct Tape Patch II. It's simple: Every time you crave a cigarette, simply slap a strip of duct tape over your mouth. The urge may not end right away, but just try to light up!

Rust Proofing with Duct Tape

Prevent your car from rusting by duct taping over the entire vehicle as soon as you get it home from the showroom floor.

Remote Control Control

Always watch YOUR favorite television shows no matter what anyone else cares to watch—duct tape the remote control to your arm.

WARNING: Hair loss potential upon removal.

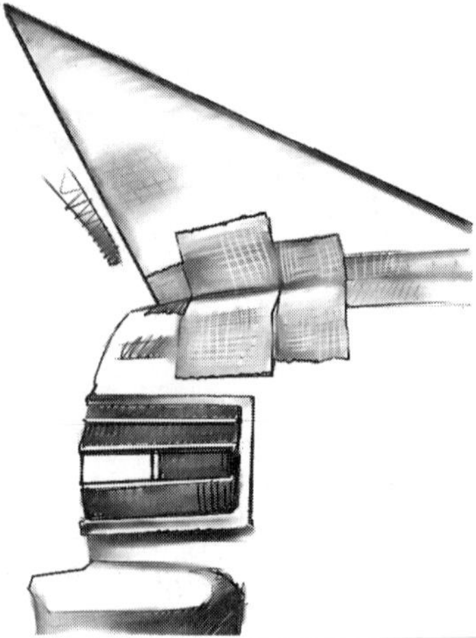

Make Your Own 50's Fins

A triangular hunk of cardboard duct taped to your back fender turns any vehicle into a stylish 50s hot rod.

Add Some Tuck and Roll

A few strips of duct tape turns ordinary old cloth car seats into fancy vinyl seats. Use contrasting colors of duct tape for that 1950s upholstery look.

Make A Ski Jacket

Here Jim and Tim demonstrate how to make a stylish ski jacket by using Bubble Wrap® and duct tape.

Let it snow!

Change Weather Patterns

It's raining again and you're starting to feel all icky inside—why not change the weather? Simply tune in the Weather Channel on your cable or satellite TV and place strips of duct tape over the screen to create your own low pressure system and chase those clouds away.

Change Male-Pattern Baldness

Cover bald spots with duct tape in your choice of color. Mix or match.

BEFORE AFTER

Want to Look Really Buff?

Duct tape floor buffing pads to your body.

Poor Man's Tanning Bed

Line the inside of a canoe with duct tape, set it out in the sun, step inside, and broil yourself until you're done.

Dozing Drooler's Delight

Apply duct tape to your pillows to cover those unsightly drool stains.

PLEASE NOTE: Sleeping drooler's head will tend to slide off an entirely duct taped pillow. To avoid this, simply duct tape the sleeper's head to the pillow.

Duct Tape Rainwear

Cover any old overcoat with duct tape to create a highly visible, heavy-duty raincoat. For the "Old Salt" look, use bright yellow duct tape.

Novice Duct Tape Handling Tip #1: Do not attempt to use duct tape on wet surfaces, or handle it with wet hands (moisture is duct tape's arch-nemesis)

Jim and Tim ask Did You Know?

If scientists decided to mark the equator with a line of duct tape (to make it easier to identify from airplanes and satellites), they would need 582,396 seventy-five-yard rolls and a whole lot of spare time to cover all 24,818 miles.

If you wanted to build a duct tape ladder to the moon, it would take 5,606,983 seventy-five-yard rolls just to make one of the 238,900-mile vertical supports.

Duct Tape Makes Shopping Safe

Stop worrying about losing your kid in public: Tether your child to your side while shopping. Simply fold a length of tape in half, fasten one end loosely around your child's wrist, and secure the other end around your waist.

Jim's wife tethers him to the parking meter so she can shop without worrying about him wandering off to the duct tape section all the time.

Shut up, Tim!

3

Duct Tape Clergy

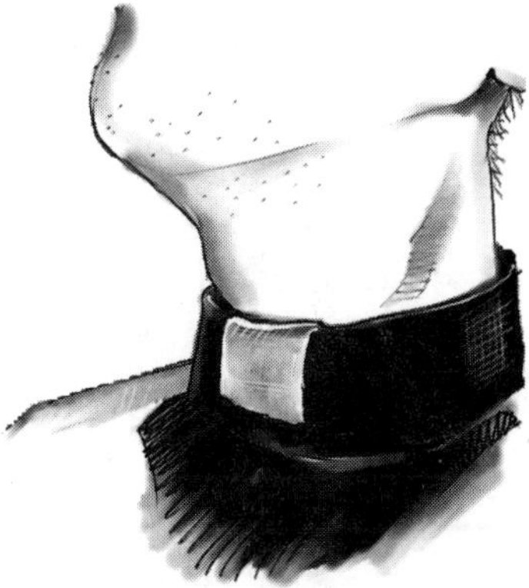

So you went ahead and became an ordained minister through that classified ad in the back of *Rolling Stone Magazine,* but no one believes you? Create your own clerical collar with black and white duct tape for that air of authenticity.

Airport Workers' Ear Saver

Duct tape over the hole on one side of two empty duct tape rolls, then duct tape one over each ear—makes a great sound buffer! For added sound protection, fill with popcorn.

NOTE: Also works great for parents with a colicky infant.

Duct Tape Twins

Parents of twins? Pay for all those diapers by earning extra money on the carnival circuit: Duct tape your twosome back-to-back and you'll have the most unique set of Siamese twins to ever grace the side show.

Creative Lighting

Turn any floor or table lamp into a ceiling fixture—just duct tape it upside-down to the ceiling.

NOTE: Duct tape is also good for hiding and securing unsightly lamp cords.

Hide Your Dough Near Your Buns

Avoid pickpockets by using duct tape to secure your wallet to your buttocks.

Arthritis Relief

We've heard that copper can relieve some of your arthritis pain. So make use of those pennies in your junk drawer—duct tape them to your arthritic joints.

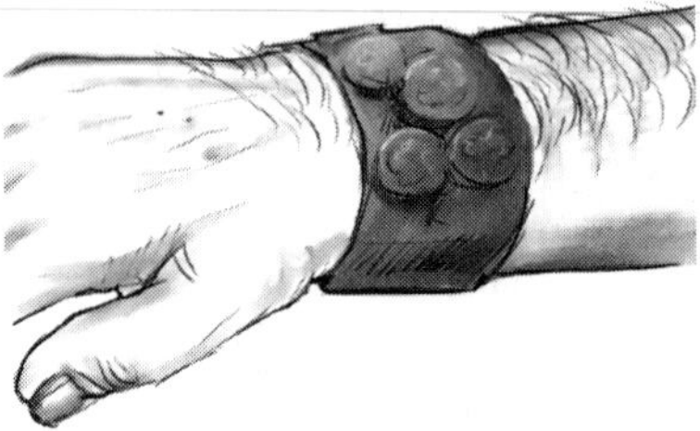

Make a Perma Lunch Bag

Jim and Tim are turning an ordinary paper lunch bag into a perma lunch bag by covering it with duct tape.

Your kid will be the envy of the whole school!

Wheelbarrow Liner

Line the bed of your wheelbarrow with duct tape and it won't rust when you leave it out in the elements. Line it with duct tape sticky-side-out and it will be a lot easier for you to haul chicken feathers.

Duct Tape Limousine

Make your car into a limo by cutting it in half and duct taping two-by-fours and plywood between the front and rear ends. Cover the wood with duct tape.

Static-Free Reception

Duct tape dryer sheets to your antennae for static-free reception.

Using Kids for Better TV Reception

Ensure good TV reception without an expensive rooftop antenna or cable—have the kids move the rabbit ears until your picture comes in perfect, then just tape the kids in place. (If they start whining, remind them that you are allowing them to stay up past their bedtime to watch—or at least listen to—the TV.)

Cut Costs on that Living Room Makeover

Replace old vertical blinds with double-length strips of duct tape folded back upon themselves and hang them using your old hardware. Your new blinds will be durable, UV-fading resistant, and will wipe clean with a damp sponge.

Save Time Cleaning

Duct tape a garbage bag to the back of your vacuum cleaner and you won't have to change bags so often.

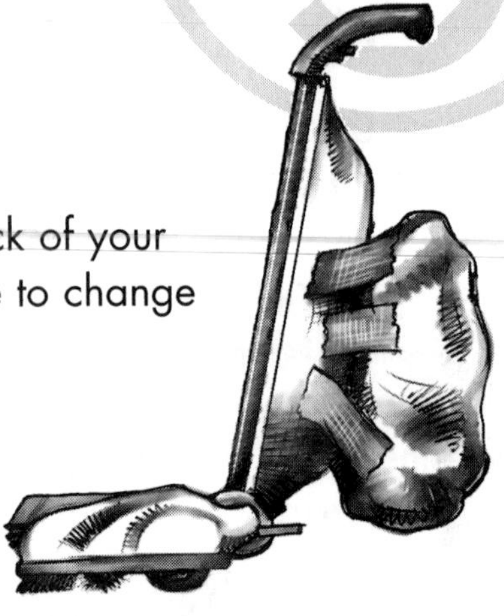

Jim and Tim ask Did You Know?

The average plumber charges over $40 per hour for a service call while the average seventy-five-yard roll of quality duct tape costs less than $6. Something to think about.

Even though Jim & Tim call it "The Ultimate Power Tool," duct tape is not really a power tool.

Not in the sense that you plug it in.
Right, Tim. But it is a power tool in the sense of what a powerful tool it is.
Yeah, I know. I just hope no one was looking for a power cord on a roll of duct tape just because of something we said.

Novice Duct Tape Handling Tip #2:
Do not attempt to cut duct tape with a scissors—it will get all gummed up and stuck to itself. You should be able to rip it easily by hand.

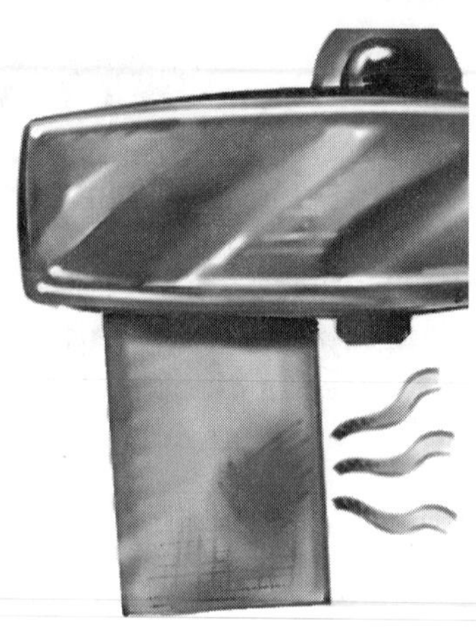

Good-Bye Pine Tree Hello Duct Tape

Put a little cologne on a strip of duct tape and stick it on your car's rear-view mirror: Instant air freshener.

No More Spilled Milk

Avoid those inevitable spills at the dinner table: Duct tape your beverages to the table and drink from straws.

3

Train Your Dog

Teach your dog to heel by duct taping it to your left leg. You'll be winning obedience school awards in no time.

DTTV Satellite Dish

Impress your neighbors with your very own direct TV satellite dish! Just follow these easy steps:

1. Find a pizza place that makes an 18-inch pizza.
2. Order a large sausage and mushroom TO GO.
3. Eat the pizza.
4. Locate the 18-inch cardboard circle (should be just under where the pizza was).
5. Wrap the cardboard circle with duct tape.
6. Nail it to your roof so the neighbors can see it.
7. Have your shifty brother-in-law "pirate" cable from your neighbors while they're watering their lawn and admiring your new satellite dish!

Squirrel Be Gone!

Keep squirrels out of the bird feeder. Apply a wad of duct tape to the pole, sticky-side-out.

Bookends, Schmookends!

Just duct tape the volumes on either end of a row of books to each other and they'll never fall over again.

Never Wash Dishes Again!

Line your plates with duct tape before each meal, and when you've finished eating, remove the tape—and the mess—and voila! Clean dinnerware.

Long-Winded Sermon Remedy

Are the kids restless in church? A strip of duct tape placed sticky-side-up on the pew keeps them from moving around too much.

Make a Comfortable Bike Seat

Make your hard, pointy racing bike seat as comfortable as your favorite chair. Simply duct tape three or four layers of squishy foam rubber to the seat.

Ahhh!

Plumber Butt Patch

Avoid embarrassing overexposure when working under the sink.

Funny Phone

Here's a practical joke that should freak out your teenage daughter: duct tape the handset of the telephone to the base of the telephone and watch the kid frantically try and remove it as it rings.
Hours of fun for the whole family!

Duct Tape Advisory Label

Kids: slap a patch of duct tape on your newest CD and impress your friends by telling them it's covering up one of those "parental advisory" labels and you pulled a fast one on your parents.

Duct Tape Mags

Lose your chrome hubcaps? Replace them with the silvery finish of duct tape (no one will notice, and duct tape doesn't dent).

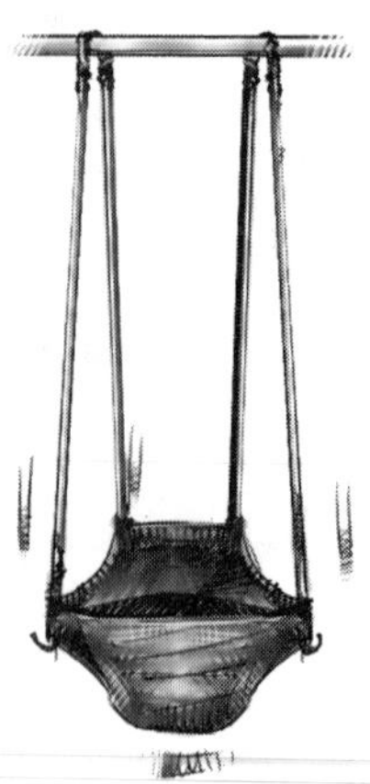

A Jump-Up for Junior

Bungee cords and duct tape combine naturally to create your own "Johnny Jump-Up" for baby.

Duct Tape Deters Toddler Tinkering

Use duct tape over unused electric outlets and to keep lower cupboard doors securely shut and prevent curious toddlers from injury, electrocution, or from finding your Victoria Secret catalogs.

advertisement

Duct Tape Abs

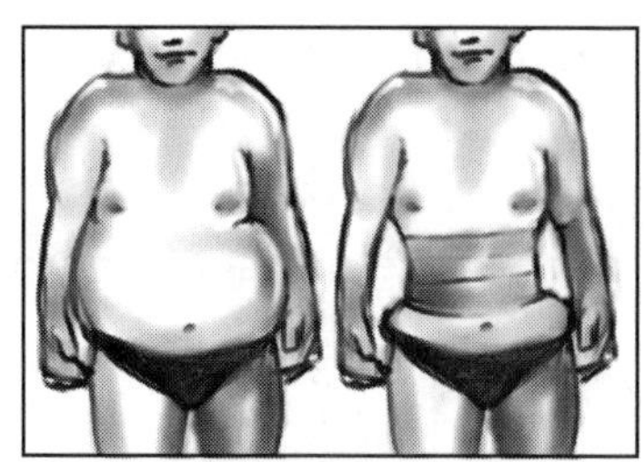

Artist's Rendering: Before and After Duct Tape Abs

The workout video that targets the tummy. Fit into your old clothes again without exercising! This full-length video guides you through proven duct taping techniques guaranteed to give you a trim waist just like the Hollywood stars!

See results in as little as 5 minutes!

Perfect for those attending their twenty-year high school reunion, or newly single adults hitting the dating circuit again.

Order today and get **Duct Tape Buns** absolutely ***free!***

Available wherever duct tape is sold.

Duct Tape Pong

Duct tape stripes on a four-by-eight sheet of plywood and erect a little duct tape net across the middle. Presto! A ping pong table!

Duct Tape Pharmaceuticals

Wrap pills in a layer of duct tape. They'll go down smoother and they'll be time-released.

Except for the Thompson's gazelle, most hoofed animals have a really hard time getting duct tape off the roll.

The Vatican reportedly goes through 17 seventy-five-yard rolls of duct tape per annum. While there is no official report on what the tape is used for, close observers have noted that not once has it been verified that the big hat has blown off the Pope's head, no matter how windy the conditions.

Novice Duct Tape Handling Tip #3:
If you allow a strip of duct tape to fall onto itself, it will stick (duh). Don't try to rescue this piece, rip a new piece and try again.

Power Boat Blow Drier

Don't know what to do with those icky wet towels after a day at the lake? Duct tape them to the sides of your boat and take a spin around the lake to dry them.

Pop Bottle Preserver

Four passengers in the boat but you only have three life preservers? No problem! Duct tape eight one-gallon air-filled-and-sealed plastic two-liter pop bottles together and duct tape the whole contraption to your chest.

Toolbox Latch

Too much duct tape in your toolbox for it to latch properly? Duct tape makes an excellent expandable latch!

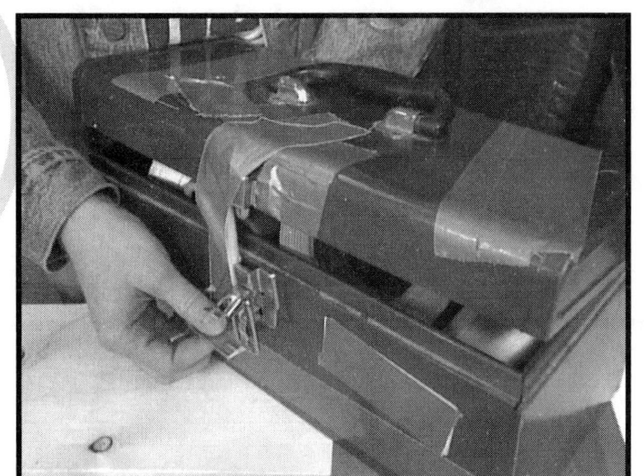

Save your Relationship

Forgetful? Write down your "things to do" list on a piece of paper, then duct tape it to your forehead. Each time you go to the bathroom, you'll inevitably look in the mirror as you wash and you'll remember what you have to do. (Be sure to write the note backwards so it reads right in the mirror reflection.)

Sniffer Snuffer

Stop the family dog from embarrassing you as he "greets" your guests: duct tape over his snout and that awkward sniffing will come to an end. (Not endorsed by the ASPCA.)

Duct Tape Depression Relief

Whenever the world starts getting you down, use duct tape to attach yourself to the bedroom ceiling. You'll get a whole new outlook on life from up there.

Duct Tape Instrumental in Preventing Accidents

Marching band tuba players: Put a few strips of duct tape over the bell and you won't have birds, squirrels, and small children accidentally falling into your tuba.

Duct Tape Mute

Trumpet players, don't panic if you left your mute at the last gig. A little duct tape across the bell and you can wah-wah the night away.

3

Keep Your Distance

Tired of people violating your "personal space"? Duct tape a hula hoop around your waist and people will be forced to keep their distance.

Travel with Sanitary Confidence

Never worry about the sanitary conditions in public restrooms again: Before you leave home, protect yourself by applying duct tape to areas of your body that may come in contact with bathroom fixtures, and relieve yourself with confidence when you're away from the house.

Win at Craps!

Apply duct tape to a pair of dice so it is sticky-side out opposite a four and three (or five and two, or six and one). Roll the dice. Voila! Instant seven!

Save the Birds' Bath

Don't throw away that cracked bird bath: dry it well, then make a duct tape patch.

3

Filmed in Ducto-Vision

Can't afford a video camera? Duct tape vacation slides side by side, then pull slides quickly in front of your eyes: home movies in stunning, high-quality 35mm!

Piano Players:

Duct tape lightly over your piano strings to create a new harmonic sound.

John Tesh:

Duct tape tightly around your piano strings to muffle the sound.

Yanni:

Close the cover over your keyboard and duct tape it shut to prevent sound.

Duct Tape Speeds Dorothy Home

Turn your old shoes into ruby slippers with the help of red duct tape. Now click your heals together three times and say, "There's no tape like duct tape!"

Real Rover Appeal

So your girlfriend would like you better if her dog liked you? Simple solution: duct tape a flank steak to your chin.

Bikers for Duct Tape

Cover any old jacket with black duct tape and you've got one mean-looking biker's jacket.

Restaurant Prank

Unscrew the top of salt and pepper shakers, duct tape over the opening, and screw the lids back on.

Duct Tape Swimsuit

Feel like a lunch-hour swim but forgot your suit? No problem! Duct tape = Speedos-on-a-Roll.
WARNING: Hair removal *will* occur. If this is not desired, coat yourself with petroleum-based lubricant prior to taping.

Better Eating with Duct Tape

Duct tape a fork and spoon together:
You've just made your very own spork!

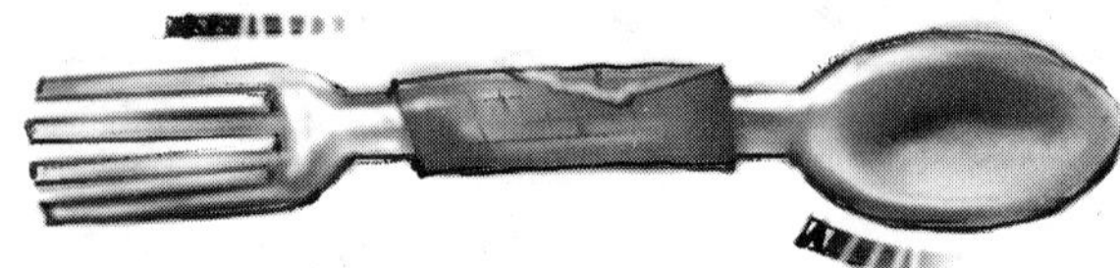

Stay-Put Pen

Retailers: Sick of customers always walking off with your pen after they write a check? Duct tape it to the counter.

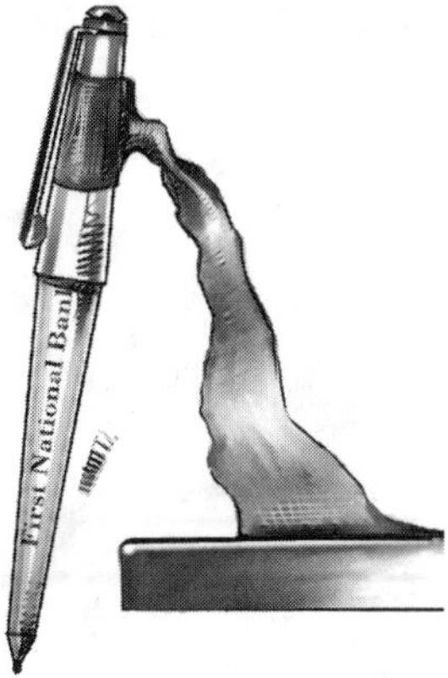

Another Option

Convenience store operators: If you duct tape plastic spoons to pens to prevent them from being stolen, get serious! Duct tape a toilet plunger to the pen—they'll NEVER take it!

3

Cookin' with Duct Tape

Duct tape a bottle of vinegar to a bottle of honey, remove lids, pour: Homemade sweet and sour sauce.

Anti-Chap Tape

Protect yourself against really bad cases of chapped lips. Simply tape over each lip.

Duct Tape Chopper Stopper

Sick of paying high prices for denture adhesive? Next time your teeth start to slip, tape that bridge in place and have at those apples!

NOTE: Works best if you can somehow dry out your gums before application.

Why Did the Chicken . . .

Duct tape some chicken feed to the other side of the road—that will answer the age-old question once and for all!

Duct Tape V-Chip

Parents: no need to wait for the V-Chip to control your children's television viewing privileges. Just tune in a kid-appropriate channel and duct tape over the infrared signal on the remote control. If they manage to take the duct tape off, next time just duct tape the remote to the ceiling.

Cell Phone Safety

Safety first when driving!
Duct taping your cell phone to the side of your face keeps both hands free for the steering wheel.

And Now, Hair's the News

Have you always wanted "newscaster-perfect" hair like Tom Brokow? Try fashioning a black or brown duct tape toupee. Or go with classic gray or white duct tape for the "Ted Baxter" look.

Duct Tape Bottom Buffer

When attending sporting events at outdoor stadiums with hard (and sometimes cold) bleacher seats, duct tape pillows to your posterior to prevent a sore or icy tush.

The average American annually eats over 100 pounds of pork products and produces several tons of garbage, yet requires only 2.6 seventy-five-yard rolls of duct tape to survive.

ABC's "Nightline" uses over twenty rolls of duct tape each year just to keep Ted Koppel's hairpiece in place.

Novice Duct Tape Handling Tip #4:
If stacking duct tape rolls, put a sheet of wax paper between the rolls (especially in hot garages). This will prevent the duct tape rolls from fusing together.

Overzealous Environmentalists

You don't have to scare away friends just because you don't believe in antiperspirant.
Duct tape under your armpits: it's effective, stain-stopping, and what could be more natural?

Norwegian Diet Dilemma Defused

Unexpected guests from Norway and you're out of lefse? Simply substitute with duct tape—it has the same texture and a lot more flavor!

Made in the Shade

A palm tree duct taped to your back keeps you in the shade no matter where you are.

Duct Tape Rain Apparel

Sudden cloudburst threatening your golf game? Duct tape over your sweater for a weatherproof rain slicker.

You are Never Lost with Duct Tape

Prevent getting lost no matter how far you roam: Duct tape a sign reading "you are here" to your chest so you'll always know exactly where you are.

Oktoberfest Apparel

You can't polka properly if you're not wearing lederhosen! Wrap an old pair of Bermuda shorts in brown duct tape and hold them up with brown duct tape suspenders. Complete the ensemble with one of your grandpa's hats—now you just need a feather and a thirty-two ounce stein!

Cactus Picker Protection

Duct tape over hands to avoid puncture wounds. (Added benefit: Keeps your hands in good shape for flipping through the Sunday classifieds to find a better job.)

3

Sleep Late with Duct Tape

Duct tape around the bell of your alarm clock stops that annoying thing from waking you up at the same time every morning!

Emergency Airline Safety Instructions

Airplane going down? Quick! Duct tape in-flight magazines and airsickness bags together to make a parachute.

Postal Workers Safety Instructions

Two or three layers of duct tape around the pant leg prevents bad dog bites.

Cheapskate Groomsmen

Hate dishing out cash for a pair of shoes you're only going to wear at one lousy wedding? Put a layer of duct tape on the bottom of new shoes and you can return them unscuffed for your money back.

Remove a Stubborn Bulb

For stubborn light bulb removal, duct tape around your fingers sticky-side-out to help you grasp the bulb. Also protects from hot-bulb burn.

Duct Tape Book Cover

Protect your kid's textbooks and your first edition Duct Tape Books. Fold a paper bag over the cover, then duct tape over the entire cover. (Use colored duct tape for accent stripes.)

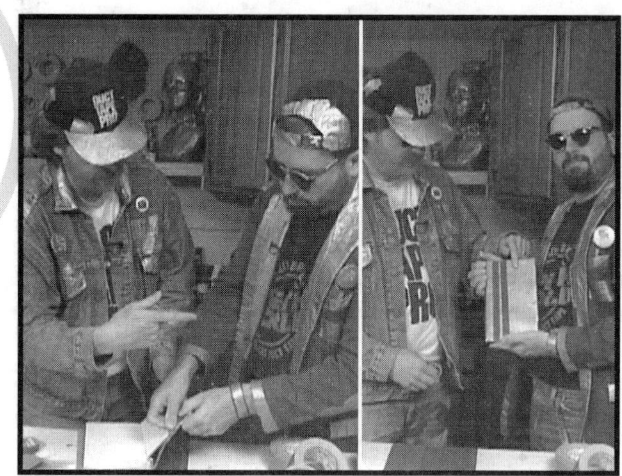

3

Do You Know Me?

Duct tape a mirror to your nose so it faces away from you. This way, whenever you meet a stranger, you will look familiar to him or her.

Banana Slippers

For the most comfortable slippers you're ever worn, duct tape a banana to the bottom of each foot. It's like walking on squashed fruit!

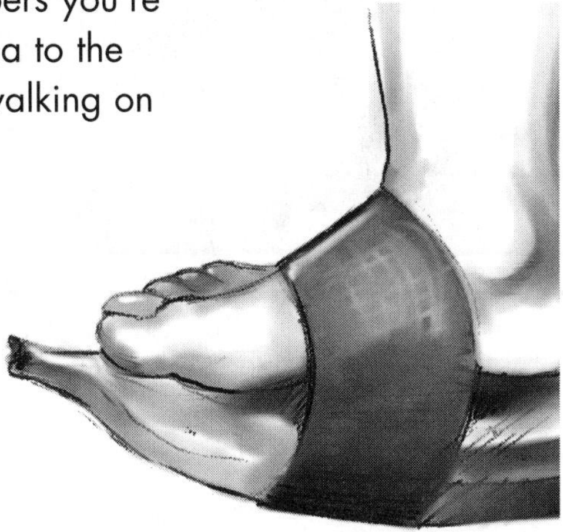

Dieting with Duct Tape

Jim and me noticed that those infomercials are full of weight-loss schemes.

Right, Tim. And some of them seem pretty silly to us.

Especially the one with that greasy little guy with the curly hair.

"Sweatin' to the Oldies" with Richards Simmons, Tim?

Yeah, that's the one. He looks like he's been swimmin' in Crisco.

So we got to thinkin', you can lose lots of weight just using duct tape.

Yeah. Read the next few pages to lose weight and save money.

Hey, Tim—I just thought of a way to lose 200 ugly pounds: Ditch my brother-in-law!

Shut up, Jim.

DIETING WITH DUCT TAPE

Day One

Depressed about your weight? Duct tape over the number window on your bathroom scale.

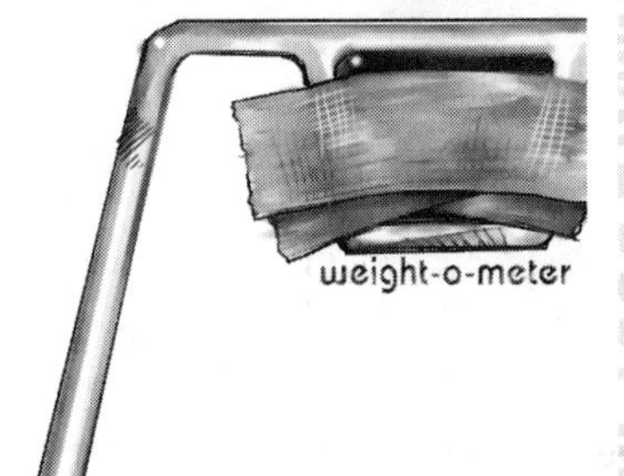
weight-o-meter

Day Two

Dining out while dieting? Duct tape over the fatty foods on the menu so you won't be tempted to order them.

DIETING WITH DUCT TAPE continued

Day Three

Concerned about fat grams and calories taking away your joy of eating? Simply duct tape over the nutritional content information on snack food packaging.

Day Four

Duct tape all of your fattening food to your kitchen ceiling and make yourself jump up to reach it. The aerobic action of this activity will burn any calories that you are about to consume.

Day Five

Finding it impossible to diet? Duct tape your refrigerator door shut.

Day Six

Still can't keep your diet? Duct tape your mouth shut.

Sock Mate Maintenance

Duct tape your socks together so you don't lose one of them in the clothes dryer.

Sock Retainer Device

Tape your socks to the inside of the washer and dryer so you won't lose both of them now that you've taped them together.

3

Chopstick Finesse

Help for the chopstick impaired. Duct tape chopsticks to your thumb and index finger.

Duct Tape Bidet

Turn an ordinary toilet into a fancy bidet. Just apply duct tape to divert the bowl's water jets so they spray up.

Duct Tape for a Brighter Tomorrow

Duct tape two 60-watt light bulbs together to make a 120-watt bulb.

Would that work, Tim?

Maybe, but you need to find a lamp with a siamese socket.

Body Taping

Body piercing is out. Body taping is in. It is much more body-friendly and speaks volumes about your sense of style.

Duct Tape: The Friendly Brand

Ranchers, here's a humane alternative to cattle identification: Design your brand with duct tape instead of hot irons.

Don't Walk

A little duct tape as a mooring stops your old, unbalanced washing machine from going for a "walk" during the spin cycle.

3

Eggstraordinarily Safe

For safe transport of eggs when camping, duct tape them together and wrap in more layers of duct tape and they won't scramble in your backpack.

Personal Air Bag

Worried about accidents while riding in someone else's car? Duct tape a balloon to your chest and you'll always have your own personal air bag deployed and ready to protect you.

Spud Wrap

Camping and forgot the foil? Wrap your potatoes in duct tape for on-the-grill baking.

3

Hands-Free Work Light

Duct tape a flashlight to any piece of headgear for a hands-free work light.

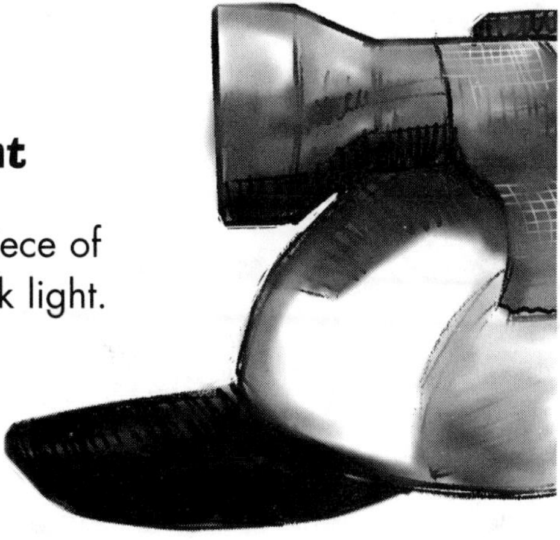

Ductamaran

Canoeing is a lot of work, and many people would rather be sailing. But who can afford a catamaran? You can! Use your paddles and duct tape to secure two canoes together, grab an old drop-cloth sheet for a sail, and you're just a mast away from sailing.

Two for the Road

Remove front wheel from bike, secure wheel-less front fork to the axle of the back wheel of another bike: "You'll look sweet upon the seat . . ."

3

Avoid Saddle Sores

Duct tape a pillow to your saddle and ride the range in comfort.

Hey, Jim. You got that idea from our Duct Tape Workshop bicycle seat cushion idea on page 25!

Sure I did, but maybe the reader doesn't have a bike!

Oh, yeah. Good thinking, Jim.

Porta-Sleeper

Save on hotel bills, rent, and mortgage payments: Simply duct tape a mattress and pillow to your back and you'll be home and in bed whenever you're ready to sleep.

Duct Tape Tattoo Removal

So you've sobered up and no longer want your "Quayle in 2000" tattoo but can't afford the expensive and painful removal process? A swath of duct tape covers your mistakes and tells the world your true political beliefs.

advertisement

Duct Tape Food Dehydrator

Avoid paying over-inflated prices for factory dehydrated foods. Now you can dry your own fruit, vegetables, beef jerky, herbs, and spices in the privacy and convenience of your own home with the ***Amazing Duct Tape Food Dehydrator 2000.*** We could charge you $59.95 for this amazing food dehydrator. But, to be perfectly honest with you, this amazing invention comes with each and every roll of duct tape you buy. Simply hang up a strip of duct tape, stick on the food, and in a couple of weeks your family will be enjoying its own home-dried foods.

Amazing!

Available wherever Duct Tape is sold.

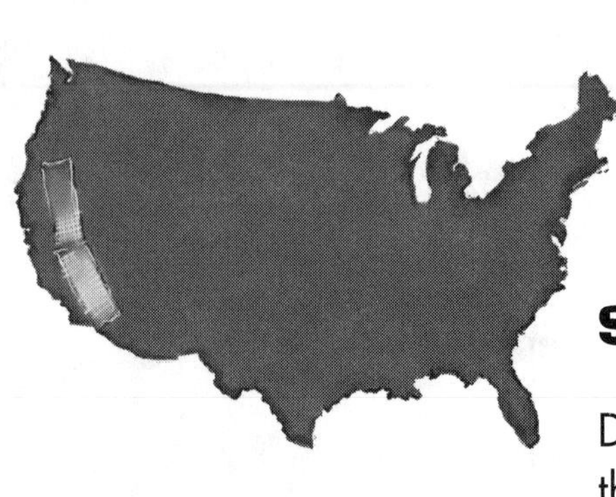

Save California

Duct tape California in place so the next earthquake won't pull it off the map.

Come to think of it, Jim, couldn't you duct tape every coastline in the world to put an end to that annoying continental drift?

Hey, good idea, Tim. Let's get to work!

Gee, You Smell Terrific!

Out of deodorant? Duct tape a flower under each arm.

A Crumby Idea

Fancy-schmancy restaurants can make "crumbing" the table faster and less pretentious by wrapping table attendants' hands sticky-side-out with duct tape.

Personalized Plates

Envious of your neighbor's personalized license plate but can't afford your own? Simply use duct tape to alter the letters and numbers on your existing plate and soon you'll be stylin' down the road.

Is that legal, Jim?

I don't know. Let's ask this police officer flagging us over.

Novice Duct Tape Handling Tip #9: Spare the cost and spoil the job! Don't fall for cheapo rolls of duct tape—they won't stick for long or hold up under adverse conditions. Look for tighter fiber content in the middle layer for an indication of greater strength.

Jim and Tim ask Did You Know?

No animals are harmed during the testing or manufacturing of duct tape; however, muskrats tend to be quite frightened by the sound of duct tape being ripped from the roll.

The endocrine glands—which produce secretions within the body—are also known as the "ductless glands." This is because secretions are wet, and moisture is duct tape's only known enemy. So wherever endocrine glands secrete fluid, duct tape cannot stick, and that area remains "ductless." We think.

Be Prepared

Duct tape a pair of clean underwear to your thigh so you'll always be ready in case you get in an accident.

Be Seen on TV!

Always wanted to be on TV?
Duct tape a television set to the bottom of your feet.

Prevent Land Slides

Duct tape rocks to the sides of mountains.

Taco Helper

1) Wrap duct tape around your taco shell to keep the filling in.
2) Eat down to the duct tape.
3) Squeeze!

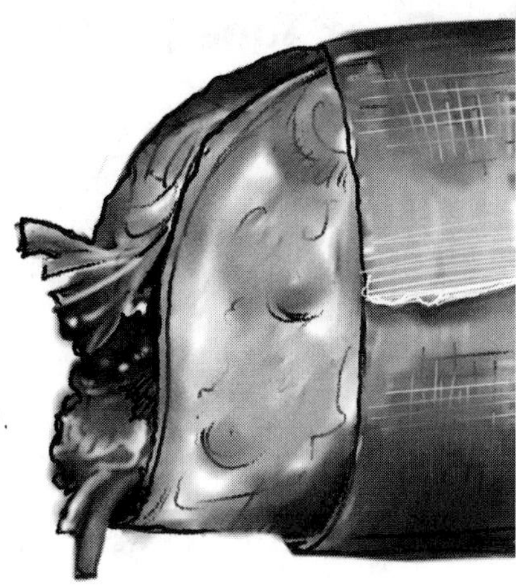

The Duct Tape Buddy System

Sick of being alone?
Duct tape someone to your side.

Sauce-Be-Gone

Duct tape over the entire front of your favorite barbecue apron. Barbecue sauce splashes will hose right off.

Use colored duct tape to make accent stripes on the apron.

3

A Safer Air Bag Alternative?

Duct tape a balloon to your steering wheel for an inexpensive air bag.
Since it's already open, no need to worry about injury caused by deployment.

Bye Bye Barney

Worried about the kids watching too much television? Limit their TV viewing: Duct tape over a significant portion of the TV screen.

Lower a Receding Hairline

Don't fret over an expanding forehead. Simply do like Tim does. Attach a strip of duct tape to the hairline, pull it down and fasten it under your chin. Now, open your mouth and that hairline comes right back into place. It's a good look. Chicks dig it.

Make Your Own Piñata!

1. Stuff candy into balloon(s).
2. Blow up balloon(s).
3. Cover balloon(s) in duct tape.
4. Hang the duct tape piñata from ceiling with a strip of duct tape.

Note: It has taken up to seventeen hours to break a duct tape balloon piñata.

Stylin' Hood Ornament

Duct tape an old bowling trophy to the hood of your car for the niftiest hood ornament this side of a Mack truck.

Winterize Any Coat

Duct tape fiberglass insulation batting to the outside of your coat.

WARNING: This stuff itches worse than wool.

No kidding. I hate that!

Why not just duct tape sheep to your coat?

That's a great idea, Tim.

According to the tenth edition of *Merriam-Webster's Collegiate Dictionary*, "duct tape" didn't officially enter the English language until 1970!

That same dictionary also points out that one definition of the word "ductile" means "capable of being fashioned into a new form." So there you have it—even it's name refers to the many, many ways duct tape can be used.

Novice Duct Tape Handling Tip #5:
Winter camping or dog sledding with duct tape? Keep the roll with you in the sleeping bag at night to keep the adhesive warm and pliable. Cold duct tape doesn't stick very well.

Post-It Alternative

We have the deepest admiration for the 3M company for turning a failed adhesive into a hot product, but can't you just write all your messages on little strips of duct tape?

Visor Organizer

Lose your garage door opener holder-thingy?
Duct tape the opener to your visor.

You can also secure maps, pens, and sunglasses to your visor using the same technology.

3

Roadkill Hair Extender

Duct tape roadkill into the back of your cap for a fashionable hair extension.

Raccoons are great for that Daniel Boone look.

Volunteer Fire Departments:

Can't afford a Dalmatian now that they're trendy?

1) Get a black lab.
2) Spray paint the lab white.
3) Cut circles from black duct tape.
4) Adhere to dog.

There you go! Not only will you be riding to fires with class, you also have a companion that can flush waterfowl and retrieve downed ducks!

3

Reversed Dalmatian

Fashion a rare "Reverse-Breed Dalmatian" by putting white duct tape spots on your black lab.

Who needs AKC papers when you have a roll of duct tape?

Fire Escape

Make an emergency exit ladder. Duct tape eighteen-inch lengths of two-by-twos (or one-inch diameter doweling) as ladder rungs and secure to window sill.

Three-Step Nose Hair Removal

1) Roll a piece of duct tape sticky-side-out around a pencil.
2) Insert in nostril, twist, close your eyes.
3) Pull fast and hard!

Sleepwalker Vacuum

Put your sleepwalking family member to work at night. Duct tape their feet sticky-side-out. When they walk around the house, they will be picking up all the crud on the floors.

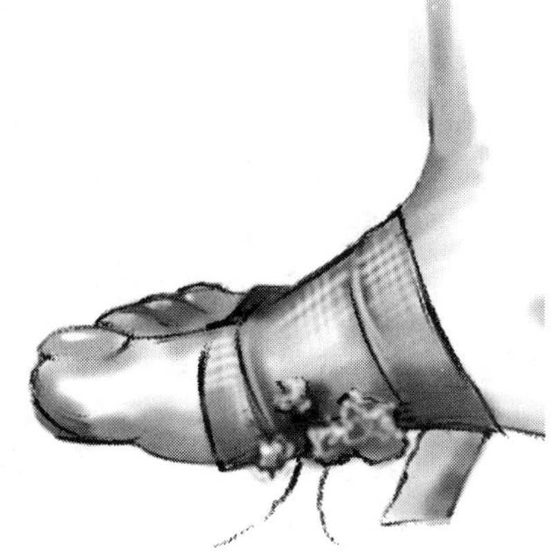

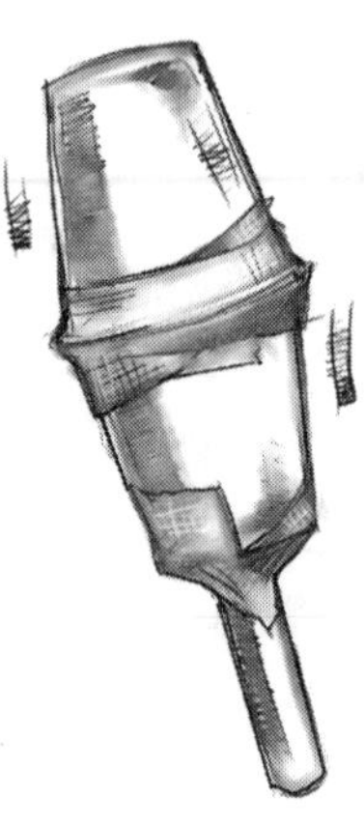

Entertain Baby

Make a baby rattle. Place dried peas or coffee beans inside two plastic cups and duct tape them mouth-to-mouth. Insert a popsicle stick for a handle.

Airport Luggage Dilemma Solved with Duct Tape

Carry-on luggage limited to one bag and you have two? Duct tape them together!

Clarinet Refurbishing

Cover your old clarinet with black duct tape and it will look shiny and new.

Solitude Refurbishing

Parents: Can't take your kid's squeaky clarinet practice anymore? Duct tape the instrument's case shut.

Danger Lurking?

Paranoid? Duct tape a mirror in front of you (facing behind you, of course) so you can always check to see if someone is sneaking up on you.

Cruise Control

Duct tape gas pedal in place once you've reached your desired highway speed: Cruise control without the extra cost.

NOTE: For an emergency accelerator release, attach a strip of duct tape from the top of the pedal to your right hand. Pull.

Be the Envy of the Campus

Need a backpack quick?
Duct tape a wastebasket to your back.

Or, try duct taping a bank deposit machine to your back. You could collect enough deposits to pay for your tuition!

3

Protect Those Peepers!

Turn any glasses into safety glasses: Duct tape over the lenses.

How will you be able to see, Jim?

Oh, yeah. Disregard this hint.

Shoo Fly

Flies in the workshop are no longer pests when you do what we do: Hang a strip of duct tape from the ceiling. Watch it collect flies. Entertain yourself for hours for the price of one short piece of duct tape.

Bachelor-Pad Chic

Time for a change, but no room in your budget? Refurnish the easy way: Saw your couch in half, use duct tape to close exposed ends and voila—sectional furniture. Cover the whole thing with colored duct tape and create trendy fifties-look retro upholstery.

Lofty Viewing

Tape your TV to the ceiling above your bed so you can watch it while lying down.

NOTE: Spare no tape when doing this job.

Bookmark

Permanently bookmark your favorite passages in your favorite book (of course, we're assuming that would be one of the Duct Tape Books).

Wash and Ride

Duct tape a five-gallon washtub to the side of your motorcycle for a quick and inexpensive sidecar.

Italian Ice Skates?

Duct tape four to six pizza cutters to the bottom of your high-top sneakers for budget-priced in-line skates. Works on the sidewalk and the ice rink!

Scope this Idea

Duct tape binoculars to a rifle for a multirange gun sight.

If Ross Perot decides once again to run for president, it could cost taxpayers millions and millions of dollars in matching campaign funds. On the other hand, it would take just one 8-inch strip of duct tape costing mere pennies to keep the diminutive Reform Party candidate's mouth shut all election season long.

Novice Duct Tape Handling Tip #6: Removing duct tape? It may leave some of the rubber adhesive on surfaces. Use a squirt of WD-40, Goo-B-Gone, or rubber cement thinner to remove the goo. (Or, you could just duct tape over the goo.)

Green-Side-Up, Sticky-Side-Out

A loop of duct tape under new sod helps to keep it in place while the roots are growing.

Save Postage

Always include a big wad of duct tape with your letters so that the envelope bulges out, then pay less expensive bulk-mail rates.

Hey, Kids! Dress Like the Hippies Did!

Instant 70s-Retro-Styles on a roll! Why pay ridiculous prices for today's designer bell bottoms when you want to look like a throwback. Take any old pair of straight leg jeans, cut the seam up the ankle, and widen with a duct tape lining.

Duct Tape Tissue

Run out of toilet paper? Reach for the duct tape and…

Wait a minute, Jim. That might really hurt.

Oh, yeah. Never mind.

Twin Engine Lawn Machine

Cut your lawn mowing time in half! Duct tape two lawn mowers together.

NOTE: Will tend to double starting time and frustration.

advertisement

The Original Duct Tape Miracle Broom

You'll have your house spic and span in no time with the cleaning product that is sweeping the nation:

The Original Duct Tape Miracle Broom

With patented Sticky-Floppy Technology!™

Each Sticky-Floppy Flapper™ can hold up to 2000 times it's own weight in dust balls and food crumbs. When it gets full, simply remove old Flappers and replace with ordinary duct tape.

Priceles$$!

Available wherever duct tape is sold.

Rolling Luggage

Don't pay high prices for those clever rolling suitcases! Simply duct tape a small toy pickup truck to a bottom corner of your suitcase. Then, attach a length of doubled-over duct tape for the towing handle. You'll be breezing through airports like a pro!

Lookin' Dapper

Fashion a nifty watch fob for your pocket watch.

Rodent Skiing

Winter time fun! Capture a squirrel, duct tape popsicle sticks to its feet, and give it a little push down a snowy hill! *Wheee!*

3

Roving Eye Disorder Cured with Duct Tape

Create your own married-guy beach blinders by taping duct tape shields to each side of your head.

Lampshade Repair

Repair or redecorate any lampshade with duct tape. Use the original silver color for the ever popular techno-modern look, or any of duct tape's many colors to match your decor.

Hair Kitty, Kitty, Kitty

Prevent hair balls on kitty with one of these handy methods:

1) Wrap cat entirely in duct tape—no hair exposed, no hair balls.
2) Use duct tape to remove hair from kitty—no hair, no hair balls!

Fetter Fido's Flapper

Does your dog's tail keep knocking over expensive vases? Duct tape that wagger in place and show off your Ming Dynasty collection without fear.

NOTE: Neither of these hints are approved by the ASPCA.

3

Sliding Door Safety

Duct tape a giant "X" on your glass patio door so your stupid brother-in-law doesn't think it's open and walk right through it.

I said I was sorry, Jim!

Cost me a LOT of money, Tim.

Swim n' Tramp

Cover your swimming pool with several layers of duct tape to transform it into a huge trampoline.

Duct Tape Dental Hygiene

Don't worry about brushing your teeth when you go out to eat—simply cover your choppers with duct tape before you order and remove it after dessert. Your pearly whites will be shining while everyone else at the table is picking the gristle out of theirs.

Another Bird-Brained Idea

Going after that "fly-away" hair look? Duct tape a couple pigeons to your head.

Fashion a Fantastic Floating Lounge

Duct tape twenty empty and sealed two-liter bottles to the underside of your old webbed recliner lawn chair: You now have a water lounger suitable for the lake or pool.

Remote Control Control II

Too many remote controls? Duct tape them into one giant remote control wad. It's a lot handier, and they won't get lost as easily either.

3

Cat Scratch Reliever

Wrap your furniture with duct tape sticky-side-out to keep cats from using it as a scratching post.

Immobilize Your Mobile Home

Tornado warnings? Duct tape your mobile home to the ground!

Golfers:

If you don't yet have your short game down and your chip shots keep rolling over the green, try adhering some duct tape "double-back" fashion to the ball. You won't get much back spin, but that baby's stickin' where she lands! (That is if the ball ever leaves your club face.)

Jim and Tim ask Did You Know?

Something to think about: Prior to World War II (the time of the "official" invention of duct tape), the world did not know personal computers, jet planes, microwave ovens, space travel, compact discs, cable television, or frozen yogurt. What would the world be like today without duct tape? It would be just like the 1930s, except the calendars would have different years on them.

Novice Duct Tape Handling Tip #7: Ripping the duct tape roll in thirds (length-wise) makes your roll last three times as long—and it's still about the width of masking tape.

Hello. My Name is...

Duct tape makes classy name tags at business meetings and conventions (particularly well-suited for Armani suits).

Another Business Hint:

Turn any tie into a power tie—just cover it with duct tape.

DUCT TAPE WORKSHOP

TV Tray Repair

Don't throw away that old, busted TV tray! Simply duct tape the broken joints and it will last you through the end of the football season.

REMEMBER: It ain't broke. It just lacks duct tape.

Grass Clipping Retrieval

Wear snowshoes covered sticky-side-out with duct tape and pick up grass clippings while you mow.

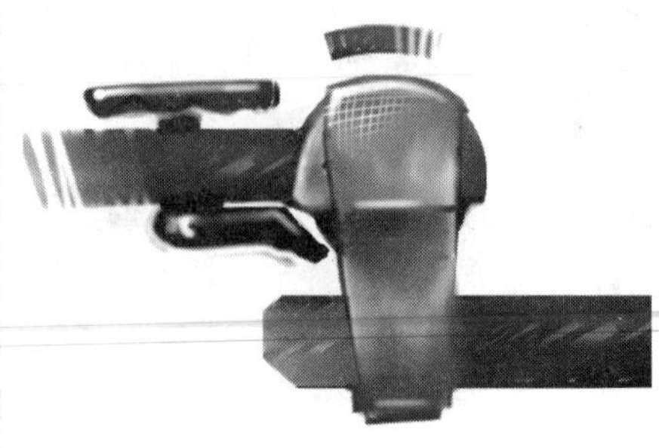

Trailer Retainer

Stop fussing over whether your ball hitch is the right size for your new trailer's tongue attachment: if they're not the same, duct tape them together.

Gardening Hint:

Speed-up spring planting: Apply seeds to a strip of duct tape first, then bury the strip of duct tape.

Hey, Tim, wouldn't this hint result in the development of super strong plants?

I'm no botanist, Jim, but it just might!

Botanist? What does your religion have to do with it?

Time Management with Duct Tape

Duct tape your daily agenda to your computer screen or dashboard so you don't miss any important appointments. Or, just duct tape OVER your daily agenda and take the day off!

Gigantic Screen Home Theatre

Use silvery gray duct tape to cover an entire living room wall, then get out your projector and show home movies on your new living room surround screen.

Duct Tape SUV

Turn any car into a trendy sport utility vehicle. Simply cut off the roof and trunk with a blowtorch and duct tape large appliance boxes into place.

But make sure you get permission from the owner first!

Right, Tim. Live and learn.

A Tip for the Postmaster General:

The next time you consider raising postage, why not make a commemorative stamp to celebrate the miracle of duct tape? If you make it out of duct tape, customers will never have to worry whether the adhesive will stick!

Dairy Farmers on a Budget

Speed up your chores by duct taping a vacuum cleaner to Bessie's udders.

> **NOTE:** If you don't have a hose attachment, make sure you disconnect that whirly floor brushing thing!

Makeshift Music Stand

Band and orchestra members: Forget your music stand? No problem! Just duct tape your music to the head of the musician sitting in front of you.

NOTE: Works best on bald performers.

A Mountainous Task

Shown on left is Jim and Tim's plan to prevent further eruptions of Mount St. Helens.

If you have faith in duct tape, you can cap mountains.

I love it when you quote scripture, Tim!

Duct Tape Shelving

Cover cheap-looking particle board with duct tape to make a really classy shelving unit. You can use your spare rolls of duct tape for the shelf supports. Or, use duct tape covered cement blocks as supports if you don't want to tie up your extra rolls of duct tape.

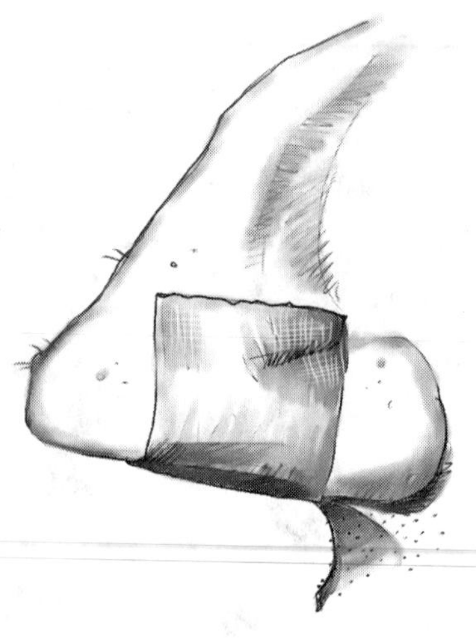

Diaper Odor Buffer

Duct tape makes an excellent nose plug when changing diapers or using an outhouse.

NOTE: Squeamish new parents may also want to apply duct tape over their eyes prior to opening up a loaded diaper.

Novice Duct Tape Handling Tip #8: Duct tape is now available in a variety of colors. However, using the original silver-gray-color duct tape is nothing to be ashamed of. In fact, most duct tape pros seem to prefer it.

Jim and Tim ask Did You Know?

Thanks to long, daily walks through the desert and his compulsive habit of covering his clothes sticky-side-out with duct tape (to stop germs from reaching his nose or mouth), Travis Jackson of Tucson, Arizona, now owns the world's largest collection of tumbleweeds.

There are reports of no less than a dozen so-called "Duct Tape Cults" throughout the world—five in Canada alone!

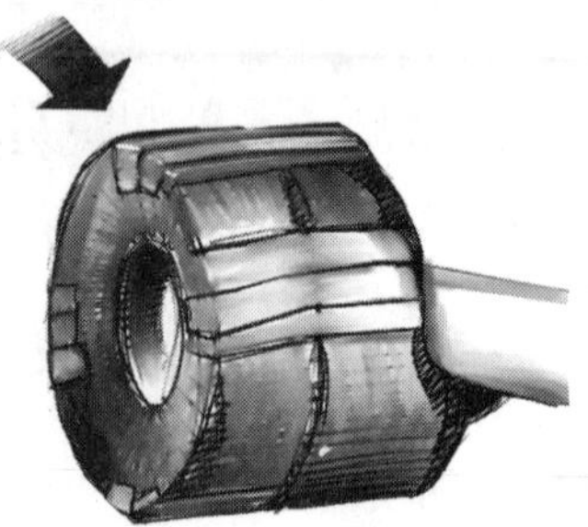

Duct Tape Tandems

Hate to change a flat tire?
Do what the big rigs do—create tandem tires by duct taping an extra tire to each wheel.

Practical Joke for Office Workers

Place a little duct tape on the bottom of a coworker's computer mouse.

Save the Nails!

Stop biting your nails:
Wrap your fingertips tightly with duct tape.

Customized Nails

Using colored duct tape as pictured creates a fashion statement:

Red for movie starlets.
Green for gardeners.
Black for Marilyn Manson wanna-bes.
Yellow for that jaundiced look.

Duct Tape Help for Fraternity Pledges

Be the life of the party. Carry on the time-honored tradition of duct taping a lampshade to your head.

One strategically placed strip of duct tape = wedgie prevention.

Kegger? Duct tape your plastic beer cup in your hand and you won't have to dish out cash for another one.

3

Bartender's Helper

Duct tape over your ice cubes so they won't dilute your drinks.

BONUS: You'll eventually end up with water-filled cubes of duct tape. A great conversation piece at any party.

Duct Tape Tanning Salon

Why spend money in tanning booths or risk skin damage by dangerous UV rays while tanning? Simply duct tape your entire body with brown duct tape for a safe, inexpensive, melanoma-free tan.

Textbook Management

Wrap duct tape around your school books for an instant back-pack. Leave it on them and you won't have to crack a book all semester!

3

Stylin' in the Rain

Seattle residents: Nothing says style and ingenuity better than an umbrella duct taped to your head. Keeps both hands free for cell phone use or holding the hand of a loved one.

Not Guilty By Reason of Duct Tape

Duct taping horns to your head dramatically increases your ability to successfully present your plea of insanity.

Duct Tape Telephone

Remember those tin can telephones you used to play with when you were a kid? Now you can make them out of duct tape rolls.

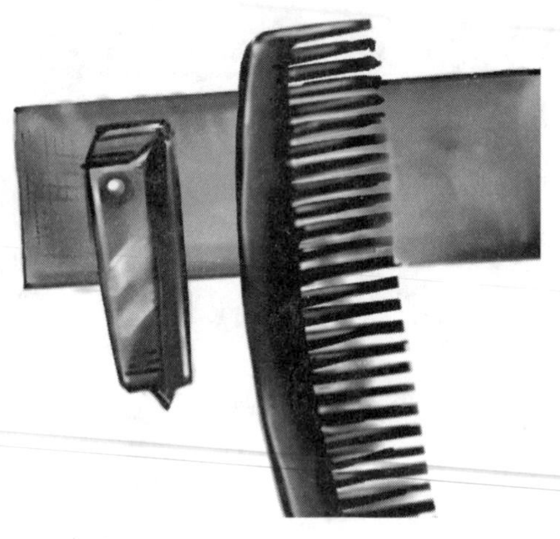

3

Bathroom Organizer

Secure a strip of duct tape, sticky-side-out, to your bathroom wall. This attractive strip stores and displays all of your personal grooming items without cluttering the counter.

Keep Bedding in Place

So you've overdried your bed's fitted sheet and it keeps popping off the corners. What are you going to do? Haven't you learned anything by now? Duct tape that baby in place!

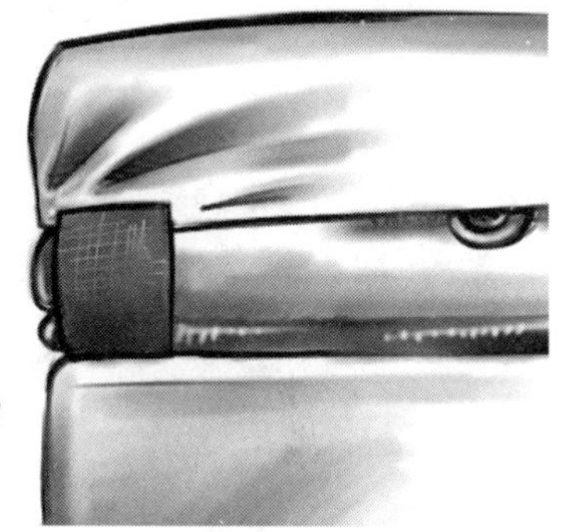

Keep Restless Sleepers in Place

Maybe your problem lies more in a restless sleeper than too-small sheets. Simply apply duct tape restraints to the sleeper.

WARNING: Doing so without sleeper's permission may result in a messy lawsuit.

Increase the Value of Your Collectibles

Tired of your collection of porcelain figurines?
Turn it into a collection of "pewter" figurines with just a few hours and a fresh roll of duct tape.

Valuable Advice for Product Manufacturers:

Add value to your product by packaging it with a small roll of duct tape and advertise that it "Comes with it's own repair kit!"

3

Catch a Few Extra Winks

Sleepy churchgoers:
Light tan-colored duct tape keeps eyes open during long sermons. Better yet, draw some "eyes" on the duct tape, apply it over your closed eyes, and catch up on your sleep.

Sidewalk Patch on a Roll

Duct tape makes a great sidewalk patch sealer. Just make sure you apply when the sidewalk is bone dry.

Obsessive-Compulsive Sufferers:

We feel your pain. Seal all of your sidewalk seams with duct tape and you will never have to worry about stepping on a crack again.

Duct Tape by Any Other Name (is just as sticky)

To be legally called "duct" tape, the tape has to meet certain heat resistance standards (if you are using duct tape on duct work, make sure it is certified). Duct tape has lots of other names, too. As a public service to Duct Tape Novices and Pros alike, here is a short list to acquaint you with some other names given to "The Ultimate Power Tool."

DUCK TAPE: Lots of folks call it "duck" tape and are scolded for misuse of the name, but history tells us that the first use of the tape (during WWII) was to keep the moisture out of ammunition cases, and since the tape was water repellent, people referred to it as DUCK tape. It wasn't until after the war that it was used on heating and air conditioning duct work and was referred to as DUCT tape. And today, Manco manufactures duct tape under the brand name Duck Tape.

GAFF TAPE (also Gaffer's Tape): This special grade of duct tape (often colored black) was developed by the entertainment industry to hold lighting equipment and cables in place and has a dull finish so that it won't reflect lights. Gaff Tape also has a specially formulated, less tacky adhesive that won't leave a residue when it is removed.

ROCK AND ROLL TAPE: Whether they can afford gaff tape or just good old black duct tape, underappreciated rock and roll roadies keep the music industry alive thanks to their love of America's favorite adhesive.

100 M.P.H. TAPE: A name recognizable, no doubt, to U.S. Army Veterans.

200 M.P.H. TAPE: Pit crews across the nation's auto-racing circuit know that duct tape holds even when you're going over 200 M.P.H. The nickname was so common, "Duck" brand duct tape manufacturer Manco has even trademarked it!

1,000 M.P.H. TAPE: The U.S. Navy uses duct tape to repair Radoms (whatever they are) on fighter aircraft. Since the planes fly so darn fast, they call it "thousand mile an hour" tape.

1,000 MILE TAPE: Norman Vaughn, arctic explorer for whom Antarctica's Mount Vaughn was named, puts it on his dog sled runners to prevent ice build-up and says it lasts 1,000 miles. He is also the one who recommends sleeping with the tape to keep the adhesive pliable in cold climates.

CANOEISTS' COMPANION: Very few canoeists would be caught without a roll of duct tape. Why? Hit a rock, rip open the hull, you're done canoeing unless you have duct tape along!

WISCONSIN PEWTER on a ROLL: Any Packer fan will tell you what's really keeping that cheese on their heads: duct tape.

MINNESOTA CHROME: In the land of lakes, snow, road salt, and rusty cars, they use duct tape a lot more often than they visit the auto body shop.

HIKERS' HELPER: Along with a good sleeping bag, a Swiss Army knife, and dry matches, duct tape makes sure outdoors enthusiasts are prepared for anything.

JESUS TAPE: In Finland and Sweden, some folks (we are told) refer to duct tape as "Jesus Tape."

PLASTIC SURGEON on ROLL: Pulls skin tight, lifts and separates—we all look better with a little bit of duct tape.

FIRST AID KIT on a ROLL: A great substitute for splints, bandages, tourniquets, sutures, etc.

Call it what you will, we still call it, **"The Ultimate Power Tool!"**
May the tape be with you!

–Jim and Tim, the Duct Tape Guys

INDEX:

The Duct Tape Trilogy

Remember, to be certified as a true Duct Tape Pro, you must own the entire set of three Duct Tape Books.

That's right, Jim. After all, it ***is*** a trilogy!

Available at your local bookstore or call

1-800-247-6789

Great gifts at only $6.95 each!

store

Jim and Tim's Duct Tape Boutique

Check out our spiffy Duct Tape Apparel and other nifty stuff approved by Jim and Tim—the Duct Tape Guys online at: **http://www.octane.com**

Not on the net? *(Don't feel bad, many Duct Tape Pros aren't.)* Send a self-addressed, stamped business envelope to:

Duct Tape Catalog
P.O. Box 130066, Roseville, MN 55113

We'll have you dressing like a Duct Tape Pro in no time! –Jim and Tim, the Duct Tape Guys